HIDING IN
DESERTS

Deborah Underwood

Heinemann Library
Chicago, Illinois

www.capstonepub.com
Visit our website to find out
more information about
Heinemann-Raintree books.

To order:

☎ Phone 800-747-4992
💻 Visit www.capstonepub.com
to browse our catalog and order online.

© 2011 Heinemann Library
an imprint of Capstone Global Library, LLC
Chicago, Illinois

Edited by Rebecca Rissman and Nancy Dickmann
Designed by Joanna Hinton Malivoire
Picture research by Tracy Cummins
Originated by Capstone Global Library

Library of Congress Cataloging-in-Publication Data
Underwood, Deborah.
  Hiding in deserts / Deborah Underwood. -- 1st ed.
    p. cm. -- (Creature camouflage)
  Includes bibliographical references and index.
  ISBN 978-1-4329-4021-8 (hc) -- ISBN 978-1-4329-4030-0
(pb) 1. Desert animals--Juvenile literature. 2. Camouflage
(Biology)--Juvenile literature. I. Title.
  QL116.U53 2010
  591.47'2--dc22
                           2009051761

Acknowledgments
The author and publisher are grateful to the following for
permission to reproduce copyright material:
Alamy pp. 13, 14 (Tom Bean), 21, 22 (Rick & Nora Bowers);
FLPA pp. 6 (Bob Gibbons), 10 (Gerard Lacz); Getty Images
pp.8 (M Schaef), 27, 28 (John Cancalosi); Minden Pictures
pp. 17, 18 (Tom Vezo); National Geographic Stock pp. 11, 12
(Mattias Klum), 15, 16 (Bruce Dale), 25, 26 (Minden Pictures/
Fred Bavendam), 29 (Michael Patricia Fogden/Minden
Pictures); Naturepl.com pp. 9 (Philippe Clement), 19, 20
(Solvin Zankl); Photo Researchers, Inc. pp. 23, 24 (Karl H.
Switak); Shutterstock pp. 4 (Map Resources), 5 (Anton Foltin),
7 (Pichugin Dmitry), cover (Luis de Almeida).

Cover photograph of a Peringueys sidewinding adder (Bitis
peringueyi) emerging from a sand dune, Namib Desert,
Namibia, reproduced with permission of Visuals Unlimited,
Inc. (Solvin Zankl).

We would like to thank Michael Bright for his invaluable help
in the preparation of this book.

Contents

Some words are printed in bold, **like this**. You can find out what they mean by looking in the glossary.

What Are Deserts Like?

Deserts are large areas of dry land. Deserts can be hot or cold. Even hot deserts can get very cold at night.

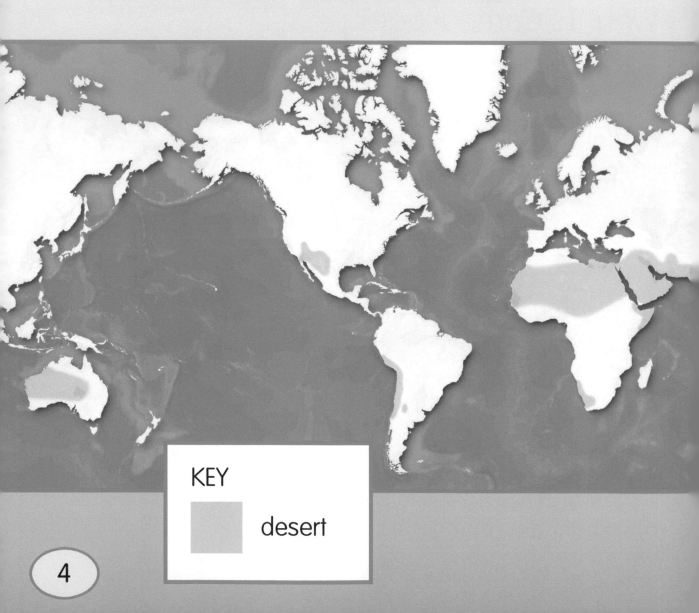

KEY

desert

A cactus survives in the desert by storing water in its **stem**.

Deserts have very little rain. Not many plants will grow in deserts. But some plants have ways to **survive** in dry deserts.

Living in a Desert

Some animals can **survive** in deserts, too. Their bodies have special **features** to help them live in deserts. These features are called **adaptations**.

The peccary (PECK-uh-ree) can get most of the water it needs from the plants it eats.

A camel has many adaptations for life in the desert.

The camel's wide feet and very long eyelashes are adaptations. Wide feet help the camel walk in deep sand. Long eyelashes help keep sand out of the camel's eyes.

What Is Camouflage?

Camouflage (KAM-uh-flaj) is an **adaptation** that helps animals hide. The color of an animal's skin, fur, or feathers may match the things around it.

The color of this thick-billed lark is the same as the rocky ground where it lives.

A stick insect is difficult to see on a branch! Can you see it?

The shape of an animal may camouflage it, too. A stick insect is the same shape and color as a stick. Why do you think animals need to hide?

Animals that eat other animals are called **predators**. **Camouflage** helps them catch food. Animals that predators eat are called **prey**. Camouflage helps prey animals hide from predators!

Bobcats eat other animals. Their spotted fur helps camouflage them as they hunt.

Find the Desert Animals

Meerkat

Meerkats sleep in underground homes called **burrows**. In the morning, they go outside to find food. The meerkats' brown fur makes it hard for predators to see them.

CAMOUFLAGED

Meerkats live in groups. They take turns watching for danger. If a meerkat spots a **predator**, it makes a special call. This call warns the other meerkats.

REVEALED

CAMOUFLAGED

Desert tortoise

Desert tortoises' (TOR-tuh-suhz) shells are gray, brown, or black. The **patterns** on the desert tortoises' shells **blend in** with the ground. This helps the turtles to hide.

Desert tortoises live in rocky or sandy places. Like meerkats, desert tortoises live underground. This keeps them out of the desert heat.

REVEALED

Scorpion

Scorpions (SKOR-pee-uhns) have hard bodies with claws. They have four pairs of legs. Scorpions' bodies **blend in** with sand and rocks.

CAMOUFLAGED

Many animals eat scorpions. Can you see how a scorpion's **camouflage** may help it to escape from **predators**—and **survive**?

REVEALED

CAMOUFLAGED

Roadrunner

Roadrunners are birds that spend most of the time on the ground. Animals such as hawks and cats hunt them. A roadrunner's feathers help it **blend in** with soil and dry grasses.

Roadrunners can run very quickly. This helps them catch their **prey**. Roadrunners eat lizards, scorpions, and small birds. Sometimes they even eat rattlesnakes!

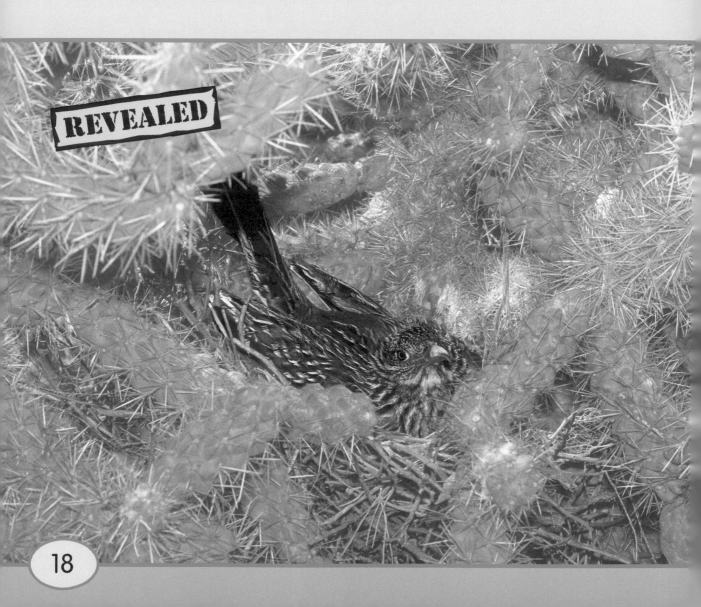

REVEALED

CAMOUFLAGED

Dwarf puff adder

Dwarf puff adders live in deserts in Africa. The **pattern** on their skin helps them to hide. They bury themselves in the sand and wait for prey.

Dwarf puff adders have eyes on top of their heads. This means they can see while they hide. When a lizard comes near, the snake slithers out for a meal.

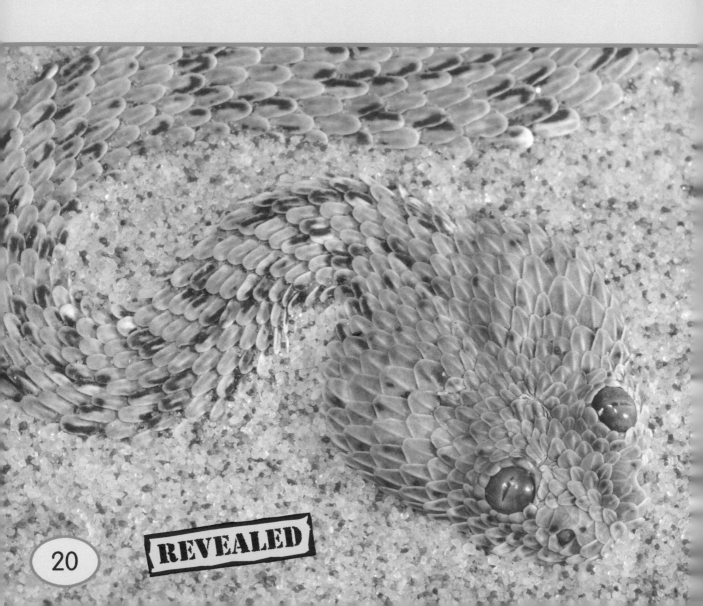

REVEALED

CAMOUFLAGED

Elf owl

Elf owls are the smallest owls in the world. They are only about five inches tall. Their gray-brown feathers help to **camouflage** them.

If an animal comes near, an elf owl may turn sideways. This hides its lighter parts. The owl may also raise its wing to hide its face.

REVEALED

African bullfrog

African bullfrogs have dull green skin. It helps them **blend in** while they wait for **prey**. It also helps them hide from birds that might eat them.

The African bullfrog is one of the largest frogs in the world. The frogs eat many different kinds of animals. Sometimes they even eat other bullfrogs! This one is cooling off and hiding in the sand.

REVEALED

Thorny devil

The thorny devil lizard is covered with sharp spikes. It looks like a desert plant. The spikes and **patterns** on its skin help it hide from hungry birds.

The thorny devil may look scary. However, it is not dangerous—unless you are an ant! Thorny devils can eat hundreds of ants in a single meal.

REVEALED

A squirrel sits on
a desert cactus.

Many desert animals have **camouflage**.
Their camouflage helps them to **survive**.
If you visit a desert, look hard. If you are
lucky, you may see some of them!

Animals that Stand Out

Not all desert animals use **camouflage**. It would be hard to miss the gila (HEE-la) monster's bright colors! This lizard has a **venomous** bite. Its colors warn other animals to stay away.

The African coral snake has bright bands of black and yellow. Why doesn't it need to hide? Like the gila monster, it has a venomous bite.

Glossary

adaptation special feature that helps an animal survive in its surroundings

blend in matches well with the things around it

burrow animal's underground home

camouflage adaptation that helps an animal blend in with the things around it

feature special part of an animal

pattern shapes and marks on an animal's skin, fur, shell, or feathers

predator animal that eats other animals

prey animal that other animals eat

stem upright part of a plant

survive stay alive

venomous something dangerous that can make you sick, or even kill you if it's injected

Find Out More

Books to read

Galko, Francine. *Desert Animals*. Chicago: Heinemann Library, 2002.

Hodge, Deborah. *Who Lives Here? Desert Animals*. Tonawanda, NY: Kids Can Press, 2008.

Wright-Frierson, Virginia. *A Desert Scrapbook: Dawn to Dusk in the Sonoran Desert*. New York, NY: Aladdin, 2002.

Websites

www.defenders.org/wildlife_and_habitat/habitat/desert.php
Defenders of Wildlife desert habitat information

www.desertmuseum.org
The Arizona-Sonora Desert Museum

www.mbgnet.net/sets/desert/index.htm
The Missouri Botanical Gardens

Index